Animal Habitats

Desert Habitats

Written by Noah Leatherland

KidHaven Publishing

Published in 2025 by
KidHaven Publishing, an Imprint of
Greenhaven Publishing, LLC
2544 Clinton St., Buffalo, NY 14224

Written by: Noah Leatherland
Edited by: Elise Carraway
Designed by: Amelia Harris

Cataloging-in-Publication Data

Names: Leatherland, Noah, 1999-.
Title: Desert habitats / Noah Leatherland.
Description: Buffalo, NY : KidHaven Publishing, 2025. | Series: Animal habitats | Includes glossary and index.
Identifiers: ISBN 9781534548213 (pbk.) | ISBN 9781534548220 (library bound) | ISBN 9781534548237 (ebook)
Subjects: LCSH: Desert animals--Juvenile literature. | Desert ecology--Juvenile literature.
Classification: LCC QL116.L43 2025 | DDC 591.754--dc23

Manufactured in the United States of America

CPSIA compliance information: Batch #CSKH25
For further information contact Greenhaven Publishing LLC at 1-844-317-7404.

Photo Credits. Images are courtesy of Shutterstock.com. With thanks to Getty Images, Thinkstock Photo and iStockphoto.
Recurring – Navalnyi, miumi, Tartila, A7880S, Beskova Ekaterina. Cover – Alexandra Lande, giedre vaitekune, Spreadthesign. 2–3 – nattanan726. 4–5 – PERO studio, Kenneth Keifer, MicroOne. 6–7 – Arnold O. A. Pinto, Shengyong Li. 8–9 – Edwin Butter, johavel, Merzougaloisirs, CC BY-SA 4.0 via Wikimedia Commons. 10–11 – Dennis W Donohue, Seth Yarkony, Ideacartoons. 12–13 – Pavel Krasensky, vektorkongen. 14–15 – Wirestock Creators, Jason Mintzer, PCH.Vector, Amanda Gravelin. 16–17 – Lauren Suryanata, Spreadthesign. 18–19 – Janine Potgieter, tratong, baby corn. 20–21 – Lauren Suryanata. 22–23 – Hans Wagemaker, Longjourneys, Pretty Vectors.

Contents

Words that look like this can be found in the glossary on page 24.

What Is a Habitat?

A habitat is where a living thing makes its home. In its habitat, a living thing will have everything it needs to survive, such as food, water, and shelter.

Deserts

Deserts are some of the harshest environments on Earth. They are places that have very little rain and can be very hot or cold. However, plants, animals, and other living things are still found there.

Dromedary Camel

Dromedary camels have long eyelashes and bushy eyebrows to keep desert sand out of their eyes. They also have thick lips to help them eat the tough, thorny plants in the desert.

Dromedary camels can be found in Southwest Asia, North Africa, and Australia.

The dromedary camel is known for the hump on its back. The hump is full of fat. When dromedary camels cannot find any food or water, they can use the fat in their hump for nourishment.

Dromedary camels only have one hump. Bactrian camels have two.

Fennec Fox

Fennec foxes are found in North Africa.

Fennec foxes have large ears that can hear their prey under the sand. Their big ears can also let out heat. This helps keep their bodies cool in the hot desert.

Fennec foxes avoid the desert heat in burrows during the day. Then, they come out at night when it is much cooler. Their thick fur stops them from getting too cold.

Hot deserts can become very cold at night.

Roadrunner

Roadrunners are birds that run a lot more than they fly. Their feet have two toes that point forward and two that point backward. This helps them run really fast across the desert.

Roadrunners are found in deserts in North and Central America.

Many animals use water to get rid of their body's waste. However, roadrunners get rid of some waste through small holes near their eyes. This lets them hang on to water and stay hydrated.

Saharan Silver Ant

Saharan silver ants get their silver color from the hairs that cover their bodies. Their shiny hairs reflect the sunlight. This helps stop the ants from getting too hot.

Saharan silver ants live in the Sahara in Africa.

Saharan silver ants only spend around 10 minutes above the ground every day. This is at the hottest time of the day when it is too hot for their predators.

Saharan silver ants work together to lift things.

Desert Iguana

Desert iguanas change color during the day. To warm up in the morning, they have darker skin because dark colors get warmer in sunlight. In the hot afternoon, their skin turns lighter to reflect heat.

darker skin in the morning

lighter skin in the afternoon

The desert iguana's scales also help it blend into its desert surroundings and hide from predators. If they need to run away, they can drop their own tails off to distract their predators.

Desert iguanas are found in North and Central America.

Deathstalker Scorpion

Deathstalker scorpions are fast creatures. They have thin legs and pincers that let them move across the desert floor very quickly. This helps them catch their prey as well as run from predators.

Deathstalker scorpions can be found in parts of Asia and North Africa.

Deathstalker scorpions are very aggressive and might find themselves fighting other creatures. Even though they are small, they have very strong venom in their stingers that can kill other desert animals.

Meerkat

Meerkats have <u>adapted</u> to live in the desert with other animals. They are immune to the venom of some snakes and scorpions, which means they are not harmed by them.

a meerkat eating a scorpion

Meerkats are found in Africa.

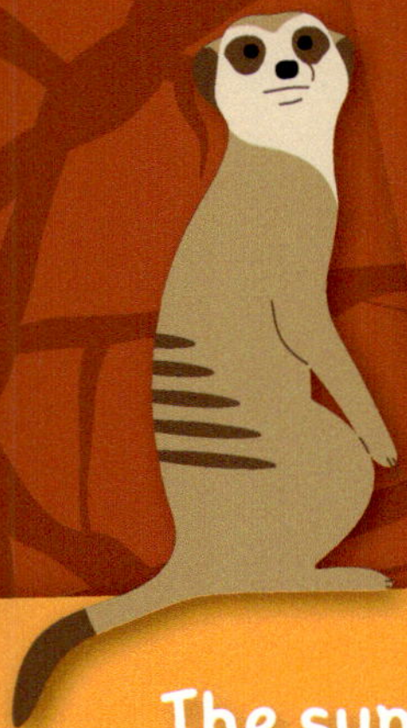

The sunshine can be very bright in deserts, which makes it hard to see. Meerkats have black fur around their eyes that stops any glare from the sun.

Meerkats stand on rocks to get a better look at their surroundings.

Jerboa

Jerboas are small creatures that stay out of the desert heat by coming out at night. They have long whiskers that help them sense their surroundings in the dark.

Jerboas stand and hop on their back legs. They have wide, hairy feet that help them jump around and stay steady on the desert sand.

Jerboas live in Asian and North African deserts.

Animal Habitats

a grassland habitat

Every habitat is home to lots of different animals. These animals have adapted to their different habitats. They have found ways to live in the environment around them.

Every habitat is important to life on Earth. Habitats might be wet, dark, sunny, hot, or cold. Keeping habitats healthy means that the animals that live in them will survive.

an ocean habitat

Glossary

adapt	to change over time to suit the environment
aggressive	likely to attack
environment	the natural world
glare	light that is a bit too bright
hydrated	having taken in enough water
nourishment	the food or drink needed to stay healthy
predators	animals that hunt other animals for food
prey	animals that are hunted by other animals for food
reflect	to bounce something back
venom	matter made in an animal's body that can harm other living things

Index

RYAN GOSLING

Making a Difference Beyond the Big Screen

By Katie Kawa

People Who Make a Difference

KidHaven PUBLISHING

Published in 2026 by
KidHaven Publishing, an Imprint of Greenhaven Publishing, LLC
2544 Clinton St.
Buffalo, NY 14224

Designer: Deanna Lepovich
Editor: Katie Kawa

Photo credits: Cover Tinseltown/Shutterstock.com; p. 5 Fred Duval/Shutterstock.com; pp. 7, 9, 11, 15, 19 Featureflash Photo Agency/Shutterstock.com; p. 13 Kathy Hutchins/Shutterstock.com; p. 17 Denis Makarenko/Shutterstock.com; p. 20 CarlaVanWagoner/Shutterstock.com; p. 21 T.Sumaetho/Shutterstock.com.

Library of Congress Cataloging-in-Publication Data

Names: Kawa, Katie author
Title: Ryan Gosling : making a difference beyond the big screen / Katie Kawa.
Description: Buffalo, New York : KidHaven Publishing, 2026. | Series: People who make a difference | Includes index.
Identifiers: LCCN 2025012407 | ISBN 9781534549685 (library binding) | ISBN 9781534549678 (paperback) | ISBN 9781534549692 (ebook)
Subjects: LCSH: Gosling, Ryan, 1980—Juvenile literature | Motion picture actors and actresses–United States–Biography–Juvenile literature | LCGFT: Biographies
Classification: LCC PN2287.G643 K39 2026 | DDC 791.4302/8092 [B]–dc23/eng/20250325
LC record available at https://lccn.loc.gov/2025012407

Printed in the United States of America

CPSIA compliance information: Batch #CSKH26: For further information contact Greenhaven Publishing LLC at 1-844-317-7404.

Please visit our website, www.greenhavenpublishing.com. For a free color catalog of all our high-quality books, call toll free 1-844-317-7404 or fax 1-844-317-7405.

CONTENTS

FINDING WHAT MATTERS

Ryan Gosling has been in the spotlight for many years. He first started performing, or showing off his talents, when he was a kid. That led to a successful **career** as an actor in movies such as *The Notebook*, *La La Land*, and *Barbie*.

Ryan's work as actor means a lot to him, but over time, he's found things that matter even more. This includes supporting causes that are close to his heart and spending time with his family. Ryan is known for his work on the big screen, but he's also learned how to make a difference beyond it.

In His Words

"I feel very lucky to have this job. I think it's one of the best jobs in the world."

— Interview for Holmes Place blog from 2016

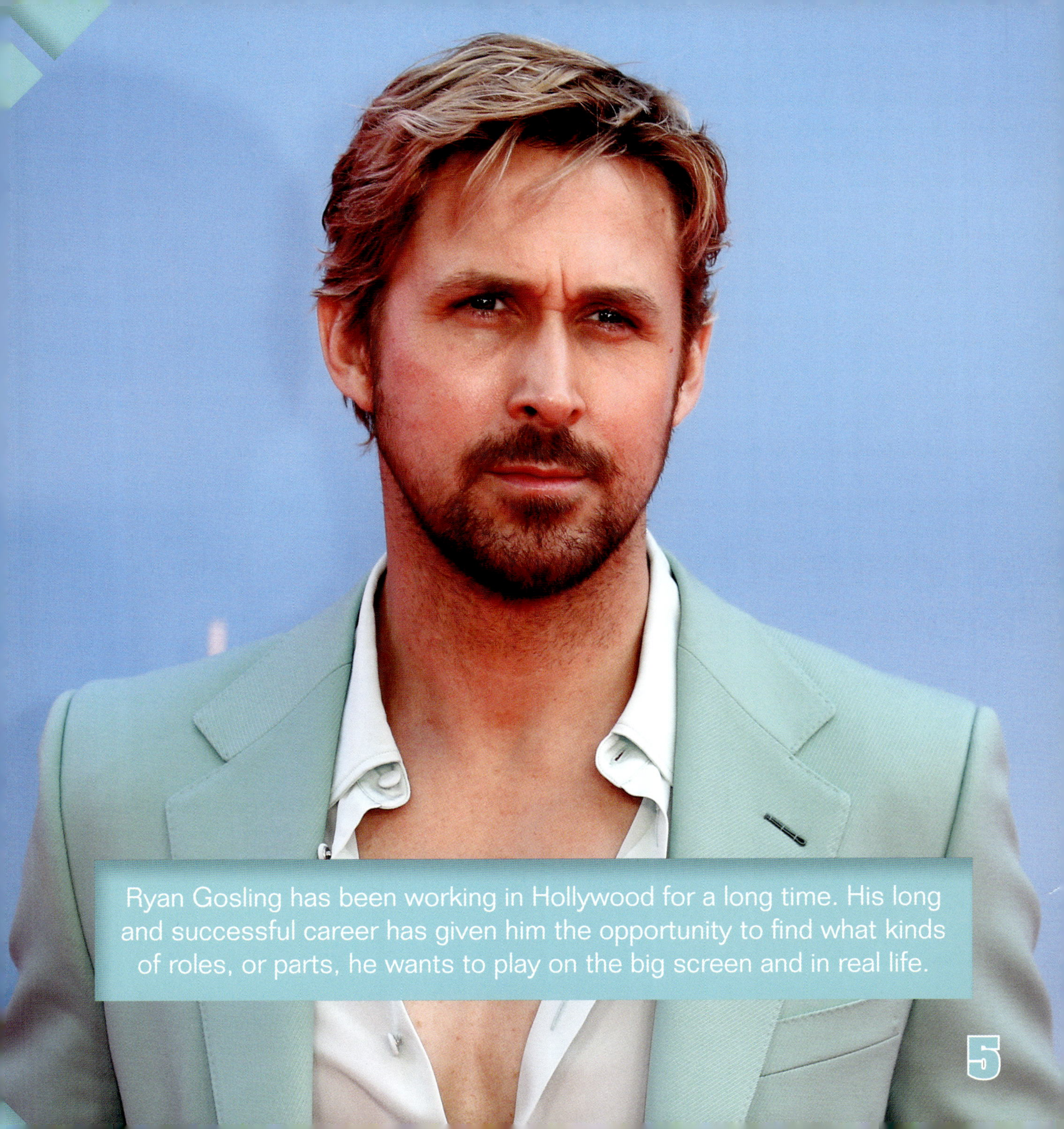

Ryan Gosling has been working in Hollywood for a long time. His long and successful career has given him the opportunity to find what kinds of roles, or parts, he wants to play on the big screen and in real life.

A CANADIAN CHILDHOOD

Ryan Gosling was born in a part of Canada called Ontario on November 12, 1980. Ryan struggled in school and had a hard time reading, but he shined onstage. He took dance classes and sang at weddings with his older sister.

Ryan's talent as a performer took him all the way to Orlando, Florida. In 1993, he began appearing on *The All-New Mickey Mouse Club* with other future superstars, including Britney Spears, Christina Aguilera, and Justin Timberlake. The show was filmed in Walt Disney World, so Ryan has said he grew up in a **theme park**!

In His Words

"He [young Ryan] didn't know what he was doing or why he was doing it, he was just doing it, and it's like, I owe my whole life to him. And I wish I had been more grateful [thankful] at the time."

— Interview with *GQ* magazine from May 2023

Ryan is shown here with his mom and his sister, Mandi. After Ryan's parents divorced, or ended their marriage, he spent most of his time with them. He's said they taught him a lot about what women have to deal with and how to treat women with respect.

EARLY ROLES

Ryan's time with *The All-New Mickey Mouse Club* ended in 1995. After that, he found work on other TV shows, including *Are You Afraid of the Dark?*, *Goosebumps*, and *Young Hercules*.

In 2000, Ryan made the leap from TV to movies with a part in the sports film *Remember the Titans*. The next year, his work in *The Believer* received a lot of **praise**. More big movie parts came Ryan's way, including ones in *The Notebook* in 2004 and *Half Nelson* in 2006. His work in *Half Nelson* earned him a **nomination** for an Academy Award—the biggest honor in the movie business.

In His Words

"Since I didn't go to school for this, all my learning has had to be on the job."

— Interview with *Gotham* magazine from October 2021

Ryan is shown here with Rachel McAdams, who acted with him in *The Notebook*. Many people enjoyed this movie's love story, and it helped make Ryan a huge star.

A LEADING MAN

Ryan was becoming one of Hollywood's most famous leading men, or star actors. In 2011, he acted with Steve Carell and Emma Stone in the popular movie *Crazy, Stupid, Love*. Ryan teamed up with Emma again in 2016 in the **musical** *La La Land*. Ryan sang, danced, and played piano in this movie. It earned him his second nomination for Best Actor at the Academy Awards.

Two years later, Ryan was praised for his work in *First Man*, playing Neil Armstrong—the first man to walk on the moon. He then took a break from the big screen and didn't return until 2022's *The Gray Man*.

In His Words

"Although I grew up watching them [musicals], I didn't think it was something I would ... have an opportunity to make. It [*La La Land*] felt special to us while we were making it."

— Interview for Holmes Place blog from 2016

Making a musical isn't easy! Ryan and Emma Stone, who's shown here with him, worked hard, and it paid off. Emma won the Academy Award for Best Actress for *La La Land*.

A HUGE HIT

Ryan's next movie was his most successful one yet. In 2023, he played the part of Ken in *Barbie*. The movie made more than $1 billion in ticket sales around the world and became a **phenomenon**. It was also nominated for many Academy Awards, including one for Ryan for Best Supporting Actor.

Ryan followed *Barbie* with *The Fall Guy*. This action movie, which also starred Emily Blunt, came out in 2024. In it, Ryan played a stuntman—the person who does the unsafe things needed to film a movie so the stars can stay safe.

In His Words

"Action films are a big part [of] why I fell in love with movies."

— Interview with *British GQ* magazine from January 2022

Fans around the world loved Ryan's work in *Barbie*. They especially enjoyed when he sang "I'm Just Ken" and danced with the other actors playing Kens.

A GIRL DAD

Barbie meant a lot to many of the people who watched it, especially women. Ryan knew this and spoke openly about his support of the film's **feminist** message and the women who got it made—its director, Greta Gerwig, and its star, Margot Robbie.

Supporting strong women isn't new for Ryan. He lived with his mom and sister while he was growing up, and now he lives with Eva Mendes, who is the mother of their two daughters. Being a good dad is very important to Ryan, and he has taken breaks from acting to spend more time with his daughters.

In His Words

"I grew up in a house run by women. I live in one now."

— Interview with the *New York Times* newspaper from July 2023

Ryan and Eva Mendes acted together in *The Place Beyond the Pines*, which came out in 2012. The couple enjoys their privacy, and they don't often appear together in public.

HELPING PEOPLE AND ANIMALS

Being a dad has helped Ryan feel like he's making a difference beyond the big screen, but he began doing that long before his daughters were born. In 2005, he traveled to Biloxi, Mississippi, after Hurricane Katrina hit the area. The huge storm caused a lot of damage, or harm, so Ryan helped clean up and rebuild in this community.

Ryan has also made a difference by fighting for animal rights. He's written letters to companies about the **treatment** of animals before they become food. He believes that all animals should be treated humanely, which means with care.

In His Words

"I've learned it's important not to limit yourself."

— Interview with *Ocean Blue World* magazine from September 2017

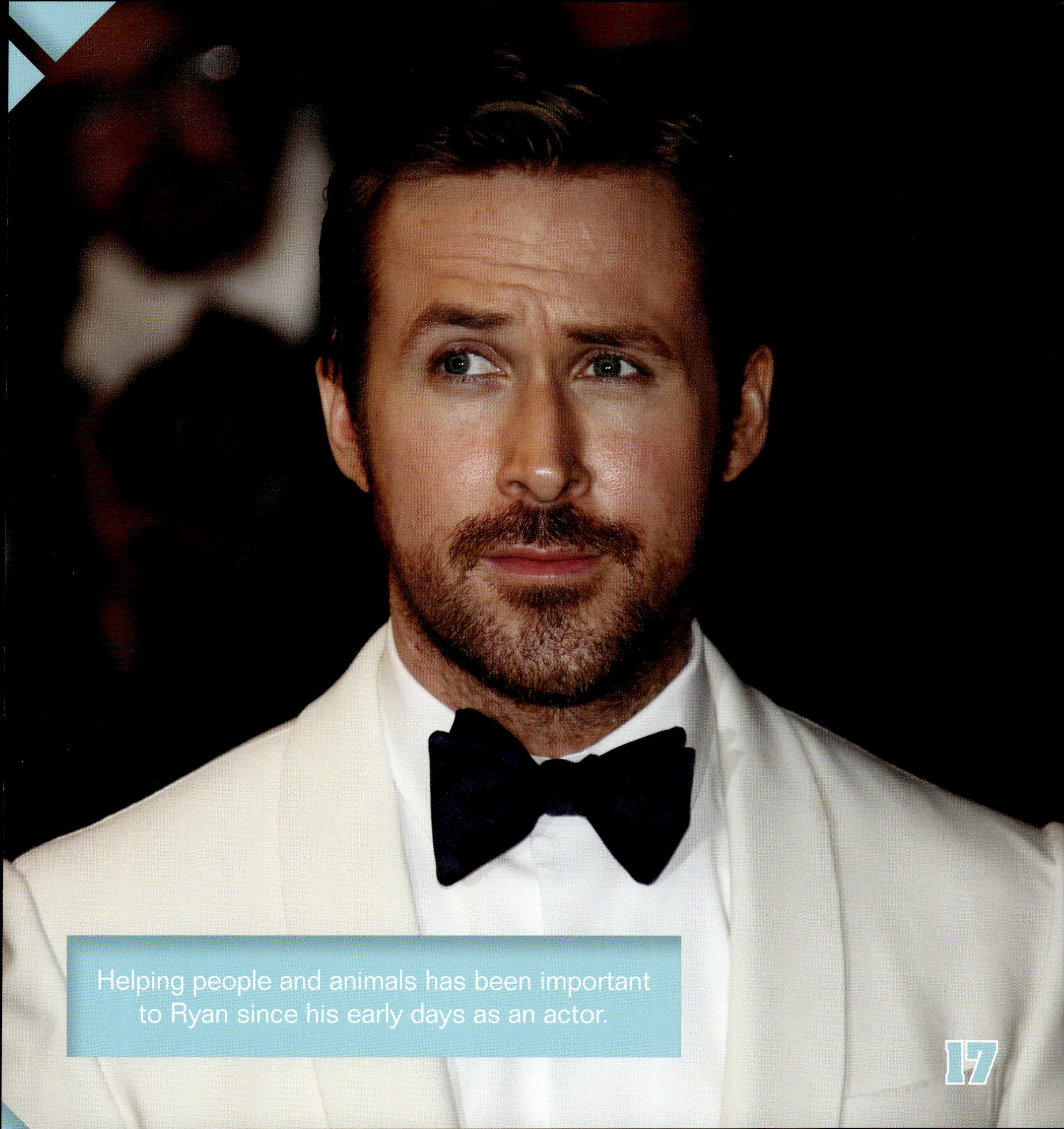

Helping people and animals has been important to Ryan since his early days as an actor.

HUMAN RIGHTS

Another cause that is close to Ryan's heart is helping people in Africa. On a trip to Chad in 2005, he saw the struggles **refugees**—especially children—were facing. He wanted to do what he could to help.

Ryan began by raising awareness of the **genocide** in a part of Sudan known as Darfur. He's worked with a group called the Enough Project, which fights for human rights around the world. Ryan has spoken to students, the press, and government leaders about this issue. He also took photos for a book about human rights in the Democratic Republic of the Congo.

In His Words

"There are ways to build personal relationships [connections] ... without having to travel all the way to Africa. It seems to me that ... people are becoming more **globally** minded ... The borders have sort of all come crashing down."

— Interview in the book *The Enough Moment: Fighting to End Africa's Worst Human Rights Crimes* (2007)

The Life of Ryan Gosling

1980
Ryan Gosling is born in Ontario, Canada, on November 12.

1993-1995
Ryan is part of *The All-New Mickey Mouse Club* TV show.

2000
Ryan appears on the big screen for the first time in the movie *Remember the Titans*.

2004
Ryan becomes a major Hollywood star after he acts in *The Notebook*.

2005
Ryan travels to Africa for the first time and becomes in involved in helping people there; he also travels to Mississippi to help after Hurricane Katrina.

2006
Half Nelson comes out, leading to Ryan's first Academy Award nomination.

2011
Ryan acts in *Crazy, Stupid, Love*.

2016
Ryan stars in *La La Land*, which becomes his second role to earn an Academy Award nomination.

2022
Ryan comes back from a break to act in *The Gray Man*.

2023
Ryan plays Ken in *Barbie*, leading to an Academy Award nomination for Best Supporting Actor.

2024
Ryan stars with Emily Blunt in *The Fall Guy*.

These are just some of the highlights of Ryan's long career as an actor. He's acted in many films, and he has plans to act in many more!

TAKING ON NEW ROLES

Ryan began working on his next movie, *Project Hail Mary*, in 2024. As one of Hollywood's most famous actors, he's in the spotlight with every new role he plays. He's found ways to use this time in the spotlight to call attention to things he believes in—whether that's the fight for human rights in Africa or the importance of supporting women in his work and his life.

Ryan is known for taking on **challenging** roles—both onscreen and off. Whether he's singing, acting, helping others, or being a dad, Ryan Gosling has shown the world that there are many ways to make a difference.

In His Words

"I don't know how much time I'm going to get, and I don't want to spend it in the wrong place. I know I'm not spending it in the wrong place if I'm with my family."

— Interview with *Variety* magazine from February 2024

Be Like Ryan Gosling!

Learn more about problems people in Africa are facing.

Raise money to support groups that help communities rebuild after storms.

Write to government leaders about the importance of standing up for human rights.

Learn more about feminism.

Support the women and girls you know. You can do this by telling them you care about them, going to their sporting events or performances, and standing up for them if someone is treating them unfairly.

When you're watching movies, think and talk about how women and men are shown onscreen and how you feel about it.

Learn more about animal rights issues, and support businesses that treat animals humanely.

Raise money for groups that fight for human rights in Africa and other parts of the world.

Ryan Gosling has found his own ways to make a difference, and so can you!

GLOSSARY

career: A period of time spent doing a job or activity.

challenging: Interesting and sometimes hard to do or figure out.

feminist: Relating to the idea that men and women should be seen and treated as equals.

genocide: The purposeful destruction of a group that is different than the group in power in a country.

global: Relating to the whole world.

musical: A movie or a play that tells a story with songs and often dancing.

nomination: The state of being chosen as one of a small group of people in the running for a prize or honor.

phenomenon: An important event that is often marked as such because it is unlike anything else.

praise: Spoken or written words about someone or something's good qualities.

refugee: A person who leaves their home country to escape danger.

theme park: An amusement park in which all the rides and other buildings are based on a central idea.

treatment: The act of treating someone or something a certain way.

FOR MORE INFORMATION

WEBSITES

The Enough Project: Ryan Gosling

enoughproject.org/upstanders/celebrity/ryan-gosling

Ryan's page on the website for the Enough Project explains the work he's done with this group to help people in Africa.

IMDb: Ryan Gosling

www.imdb.com/name/nm0331516/

The Internet Movie Database offers visitors a list of Ryan's movie and TV roles, as well as a collection of videos and news stories about the actor.

BOOKS

Mcilroy, Emma. *A Kids Book About Feminism*. New York, NY: DK Publishing, 2024.

Murray, Laura K. *The Movie Encyclopedia*. Minneapolis, MN: Abdo Reference, 2024.

Tolli, Jenna. *Standing Up for Human Rights*. Buffalo, NY: PowerKids Press, 2023.

INDEX